States
NEVADA

by Jordan Mills

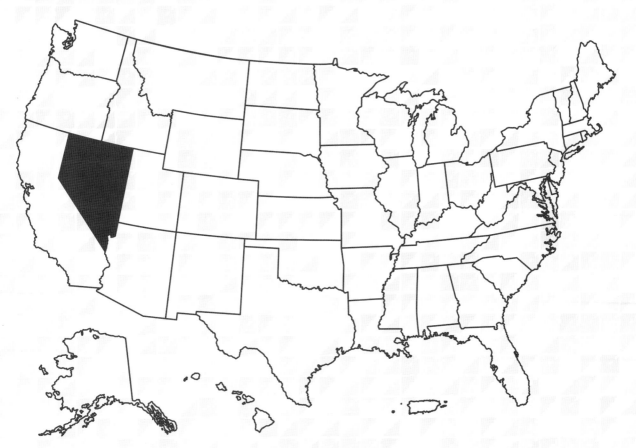

CAPSTONE PRESS
a capstone imprint

Next Page Books are published by Capstone Press,
1710 Roe Crest Drive, North Mankato, Minnesota 56003
www.mycapstone.com

Library of Congress Cataloging-in-Publication Data
Cataloging-in-publication information is on file with the Library of
Congress.
ISBN 978-1-5157-0415-7 (library binding)
ISBN 978-1-5157-0474-4 (paperback)
ISBN 978-1-5157-0526-0 (ebook PDF)

Editorial Credits
Jaclyn Jaycox, editor; Richard Korab and Katy LaVigne, designers;
Morgan Walters, media researcher; Tori Abraham, production specialist

Photo Credits
Alamy: Sueddeutsche Zeitung Photo, 28; Capstone Press: Angi Gahler,
map 4, 7; Corbis: Bettmann, bottom 18, CORBIS, 25; CriaImages.com:
Jay Robert Nash Collection, middle 18; Dreamstime: Russell Shively,
top left 21; Library of Congress: Prints and Photographs Division/
Edward S. Curtis Collection, top 19; Nevada-Landmarks: Paul Sebesta,
middle left 21; Newscom: Dennis Brack, bottom 19; North Wind Picture
Archives, 12; One Mile Up, Inc., flag, seal 23; Shutterstock: AMC
Images, 6, Andrew Zarivny, 9, Aneese, 29, Angel DiBilio, middle right
21, CREATISTA, 15, doomu, bottom right 21, enmyo, top 24, Everett
Historical, 26, Filip Fuxa, bottom left 8, Galyna Andrushko, cover,
GoBOb, top right 20, Jorg Hackemann, 14, Joseph Sohm, 13, Joy Stein,
(pine) top left 20, littleny, 5, Master1305, 17, Matt Jeppson, bottom left
21, Photo Works, top 18, Roberto Binetti, 27, Songquan Deng, 10, 16,
Steve Byland, bottom left 20, Susan Flashman, bottom 24, Tom Grundy,
7, topseller, bottom right 8, 11; U.S. Geological Survey/Nonindigenous
Aquatic Species Database/USFWS, Nevada Fish & Wildlife Office, bottom
right 20; Wikimedia: Elmer Chickering, middle 19, SkepticVK, top
right 21, Tolyab, (leaf) top left 20

All design elements by Shutterstock

Printed and bound in China.
0316/CA21600187
012016   009436F16

TABLE OF CONTENTS

Want to take your research further? Ask your librarian if your school subscribes to PebbleGo Next. If so, when you see this helpful symbol 🖱 throughout the book, log onto www.pebblegonext.com for bonus downloads and information.

LOCATION

Nevada is one of the nation's western states. It is the seventh-largest state. Most of its borders are long, straight lines. To the north are Oregon and Idaho. California lies to the west. Utah and Arizona are on the east. Nevada's southeast corner is a wavy line. This is where the Colorado River forms Nevada's border with Arizona. Carson City is the capital of Nevada. The largest cities are Las Vegas, Henderson, Reno, North Las Vegas, and Sparks.

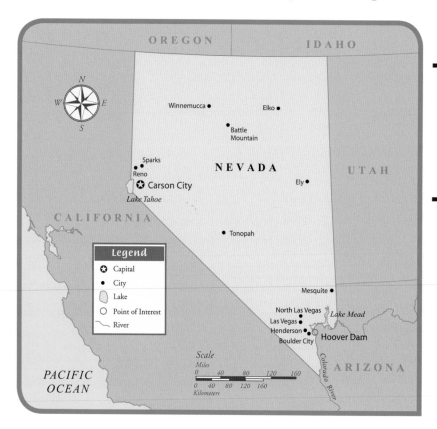

PebbleGo Next Bonus!
To print and label your own map, go to www.pebblegonext.com and search keywords:
NU MAP

Las Vegas is a popular tourist destination. More than 41 million people visit each year.

GEOGRAPHY

Nevada's land lies high above sea level. Its highest point, Boundary Peak, is 13,140 feet (4,005 meters) above sea level. Most of Nevada is in the Great Basin desert region. More than 150 mountain ranges cover this region. Wider, flatter mountains are found in northeastern Nevada. The tall Sierra Nevada line the border with California. Nevada's southern tip is part of the Mojave Desert. Much of the state is hot and dry, but there are a few wetland areas.

PebbleGo Next Bonus! To watch a video about Rhyolite Ghost Town, go to www.pebblegonext.com and search keywords:

NU VIDEO

Red Rock Canyon, in the foothills of the Spring Mountains, is a popular place for rock climbing and hiking.

Boundary Peak is found in the White Mountains, only about 0.5 mile (1 kilometer) away from the California border.

WEATHER

Nevada's weather changes often. Rainfall amounts change, bringing flooding one year and drought the next. The average January temperature is 23 degrees Fahrenheit (minus 5 degrees Celsius). The average July temperature is 76°F (24°C).

Average High and Low Temperatures (Carson City, NV)

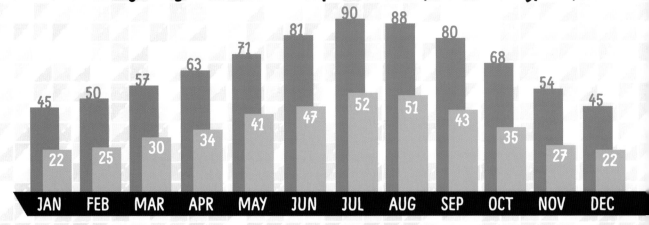

	JAN	FEB	MAR	APR	MAY	JUN	JUL	AUG	SEP	OCT	NOV	DEC
High	45	50	57	63	71	87	90	88	80	68	54	45
Low	22	25	30	34	41	47	52	51	43	35	27	22

Hoover Dam

Hoover Dam is the highest concrete arch dam in the United States. It was completed in 1935. The dam's turbines make enough energy to serve 1.3 million people.

Las Vegas

This is the most visited city in the nation. It is known for its five-star hotels, amusement rides, live entertainment shows, and casinos.

Lake Tahoe

The clear blue waters of Lake Tahoe are a popular place for people to jet ski and enjoy other outdoor activities. Millions of people travel to Lake Tahoe each year.

The discovery of silver in 1859 in Nevada brought thousands to Virginia City.

People lived in Nevada thousands of years ago. By the 1800s many American Indians had settled there, including the Shoshone, Paiute, Washoe, and Mohave. Nevada eventually became part of a large region that was claimed by Spain. This region passed to Mexico in 1821. The United States then won these lands from Mexico in 1848. In 1861 Nevada became a separate territory. It became the 36th U.S. state in 1864. The U.S. Civil War (1861–1865) was still going on then. For this reason, Nevada calls itself "Battle Born."

Nevada's state government is divided into three branches. The chief of the executive branch is the governor. This branch enforces the laws. The law-making legislature is made up of two houses. One is the 21-member Senate. The other is the 42-member Assembly. Nevada's judges and courts make up the judicial branch.

Nevada's capitol building was designed in 1870 by architect Joseph Gosling.

INDUSTRY

The tourism industry is the state's largest source of income. More than 50 million people visit Nevada each year. Many of Nevada's residents work at casinos, hotels, restaurants, shops, and other tourist attractions.

Nevada mines produce gold, silver, salt, silicate, limestone, copper, and lithium. Nevada is the nation's top producer of gold and its second-largest producer of silver.

Livestock is Nevada's main agricultural product. Sheep and cattle are raised on ranches. Nevada farmers also grow a wide variety of crops, including potatoes, alfalfa, barley, wheat, corn, oats, onions, garlic, and honey.

Visitors to Las Vegas are the biggest contributors to the state's tourism industry.

Manufacturing also provides some of the state's revenue. Several companies make stone, clay, and glass products from the minerals in Nevada. The state also produces concrete, machinery, and printed paper materials.

The northern part of Nevada leads the state in silver production.

POPULATION

Nevada has been one of the fastest-growing states in population for many years. This growth is due in part to the state's warm weather, low taxes, and high birth rate. White people are the largest group in the state. About 1.5 million white people live in Nevada. About 717,000 Nevadans are Hispanic. Asians and African-Americans each make up less than 10 percent of Nevada's population. Many of the state's American Indians belong to the Shoshone, Paiute, or Washoe groups.

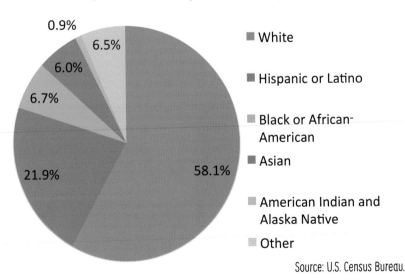

Population by Ethnicity

- 0.9%
- 6.5%
- 6.0%
- 6.7%
- 21.9%
- 58.1%

- White
- Hispanic or Latino
- Black or African-American
- Asian
- American Indian and Alaska Native
- Other

Source: U.S. Census Bureau.

FAMOUS PEOPLE

Andre Agassi (1970–) is a tennis champion who was born in Las Vegas and remains a resident of the city.

Kit Carson (1809–1868) was the scout who guided John C. Frémont's exploration of Nevada. Carson City is named for him.

Henry Comstock (1820–1870) claimed the gold and silver deposits that became the Comstock Lode.

Dat-so-la-lee (1829–1925) was a Washoe Indian woman, the last of the famed Washoe basket weavers. Her baskets were known for their beauty and symbolism.

Sarah Winnemucca Hopkins (circa 1844–1891) was a Paiute translator and author. She worked for peace and Indian rights. Hopkins wrote *Life Among the Paiutes: Their Wrongs and Claims* (1883).

Pat Nixon (1912–1993) was the wife of President Richard Nixon. She was born as Thelma Catherine Ryan in Ely.

STATE SYMBOLS

Tree
single leaf piñon and bristlecone pine

Flower
sagebrush

Bird
mountain bluebird

Fish
Lahontan cutthroat trout

PebbleGo Next Bonus! To make a favorite dessert of Nevada's former governor, Bob Miller, go to www.pebblegonext.com and search keywords: **NU RECIPE**

Fossil

Ichthyosaur

Grass

Indian ricegrass

Gemstone

black fire opal

Animal

desert bighorn sheep

Reptile

desert tortoise

Metal

silver

FAST FACTS

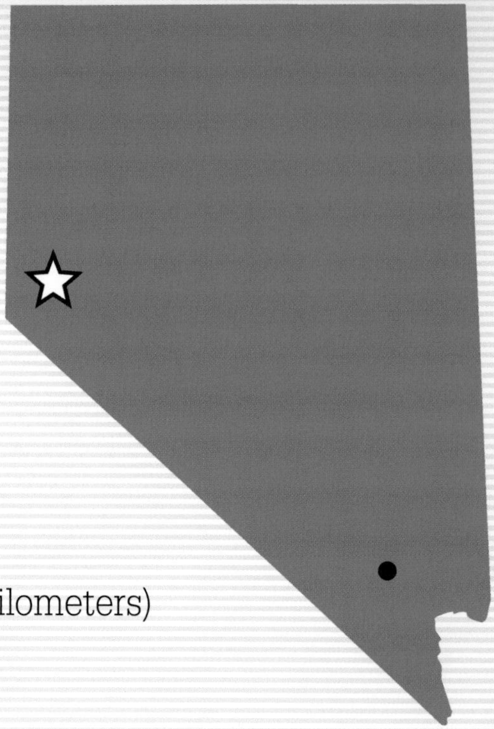

STATEHOOD
1864

CAPITAL ☆
Carson City

LARGEST CITY ●
Las Vegas

SIZE
109,781 square miles (284,331 square kilometers)
land area (2010 U.S. Census Bureau)

POPULATION
2,790,136 (2013 U.S. Census estimate)

STATE NICKNAME
The Silver State

STATE MOTTO
"All for Our Country"

STATE SEAL

The importance of agriculture, mining, transportation, and communication are reflected in Nevada's state seal. A bundle of wheat, a sickle, and a plow represent agriculture. A miner pulling a load of ore with his team of horses stands for the state's mining history. A train and a line of telegraph poles at the base of the mountains represent transportation and communication.

STATE FLAG

Nevada's flag has changed several times since the first flag was adopted in 1905. Today Nevada's flag is dark blue. In the flag's upper left corner, the words "Battle Born" are on a gold ribbon. These words reflect Nevada's statehood during the Civil War. A silver star, the state's name, and a wreath of sagebrush are below the ribbon. The silver star represents Nevada's silver mines. Sagebrush is the state flower.

MINING PRODUCTS

Gold, copper, silver, lime, barite, diatomite, granite, gypsum, lithium carbonate, magnesite, sand and gravel

MANUFACTURED GOODS

food products, computers and electronic equipment, fabricated metal products, plastics and rubber products, chemicals, printed materials, machinery, transportation equipment

FARM PRODUCTS

hay, potatoes, dairy products, beef cattle, sheep

PebbleGo Next Bonus! To learn the lyrics to the state song, go to www.pebblegonext.com and search keywords:

NU SONG

NEVADA TIMELINE

1200s
Francisco Vásquez de Coronado claims southwestern North America for Spain. His group meets the Pawnee, Omaha, Ponca, and other American Indians.

1620
The Pilgrims establish a colony in the New World in present-day Massachusetts.

1776
Francisco Garcés, who may be the first European in Nevada, travels through Mexico and Nevada.

1821
Nevada becomes part of Mexico.

1843–1845

Americans Kit Carson and John Frémont explore much of Nevada for the United States, naming many of the rivers and land features in the state.

1848

Nevada becomes U.S. land after the Mexican War (1846–1848).

1859

Silver is discovered in Virginia City, and a mining rush begins.

1861

The United States creates the Nevada Territory.

1861–1865

The Union and the Confederacy fight the Civil War. Although not yet a state, Nevada sends troops to fight for the Union.

1864

Nevada becomes the 36th state on October 31.

1909

Gambling is outlawed in Nevada.

1914–1918

World War I is fought; the United States enters the war in 1917.

1931

Nevada makes gambling legal as a way to help the state's economy. Nevada's economy cannot be supported by just ranching and mining, especially after the Great Depression (1929–1939) leaves many people in Nevada without jobs.

1935

Hoover Dam is completed. The dam stops and collects water from the Colorado River and forms Lake Mead, the largest artificial lake in the nation. Hard hats for construction workers are invented for the workers who build this dam.

1939–1945

World War II is fought; the United States enters the war in 1941.

1951 The U.S. government begins testing atomic bombs in southern Nevada.

1986 Great Basin National Park becomes Nevada's first national park.

2014 The High Roller opens in Las Vegas. At 550 feet (168 m) tall, it's the world's tallest Ferris wheel.

2015 The first-ever scale model of the solar system is built in the Black Rock desert in Nevada.

Glossary

artificial *(ar-tuh-FI-shuhl)*—made by people

atomic bomb *(uh-TAH-mik BOM)*—a powerful explosive that destroys large areas; atomic bombs leave behind harmful elements called radiation

casino *(kuh-SEE-noh)*—a place where adults gamble

executive *(ig-ZE-kyuh-tiv)*—the branch of government that makes sure laws are followed

industry *(IN-duh-stree)*—a business which produces a product or provides a service

judicial *(joo-DISH-uhl)*—to do with the branch of government that explains and interprets the laws

legislature *(LEJ-iss-lay-chur)*—a group of elected officials who have the power to make or change laws for a country or state

mineral *(MIN-ur-uhl)*—a substance found in nature that is not made by a plant or animal

territory *(TER-uh-tor-ee)*—an area under the control of a country

tourism *(TOOR-i-zuhm)*—the business of taking care of visitors to a country or place

turbine *(TUR-bine)*—a machine with blades that can be turned by a moving fluid such as steam or water

Read More

Felix, Rebecca. *What's Great About Nevada?* Our Great States. Minneapolis: Lerner Publications, 2016.

Ganeri, Anita. *United States of America: A Benjamin Blog and His Inquisitive Dog Guide.* Country Guides. Chicago: Heinemann Raintree, 2015.

Hicks, Terry Allan. *Nevada.* It's My State! New York: Cavendish Square Publishing, 2016.

Internet Sites

FactHound offers a safe, fun way to find Internet sites related to this book. All of the sites on FactHound have been researched by our staff.

Here's all you do:

Visit *www.facthound.com*

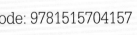

Type in this code: 9781515704157

Check out projects, games and lots more at
www.capstonekids.com

Critical Thinking Using the Common Core

1. Which of Nevada's three landmarks listed in this book would you most like to visit and why? (Integration of Knowledge and Ideas)

2. By the 1800s many American Indians had settled in Nevada. Which American Indian tribes settled there? (Key Ideas and Details)

3. The U.S. government began testing atomic bombs in southern Nevada in 1951. What is an atomic bomb? (Craft and Structure)

Index